Imagine ¹

WORKBOOK

Katherine Bilsborough

Steve Bilsborough

COURSE CONSULTANTS

Elaine Boyd

Paul Dummett

T0349578

NATIONAL GEOGRAPHIC
LEARNING

Australia • Brazil • Canada • Mexico • Singapore • United Kingdom • United States

NATIONAL GEOGRAPHIC LEARNING

National Geographic Learning,
a Cengage Company

***Imagine* 1 Workbook**

Authors: Katherine Bilsborough, Steve Bilsborough

Course Consultants: Elaine Boyd, Paul Dummett

Publisher: Rachael Gibbon

Executive Editor: Joanna Freer

Project Manager: Samantha Grey

Editorial Assistant: Polly McLachlan

Director of Global Marketing: Ian Martin

Product Marketing Manager: Fernanda De Oliveira

Heads of Strategic Marketing:

  Charlotte Ellis (Europe, Middle East and Africa)

  Justin Kaley (Asia and Greater China)

  Irina Pereyra (Latin America)

Senior Content Project Manager: Beth McNally

Senior Media Researcher: Leila Hishmeh

Senior Art Director: Brenda Carmichael

Operations Support: Rebecca G. Barbush, Hayley Chwazik-Gee

Manufacturing Manager: Eyvett Davis

Composition: Composure

For permission to use material from this text or product, submit all requests online at **cengage.com/permissions**
Further permissions questions can be emailed to
permissionrequest@cengage.com

ISBN: 978-0-357-91182-2

National Geographic Learning
Cheriton House, North Way,
Andover, Hampshire, SP10 5BE
United Kingdom

Locate your local office at **international.cengage.com/region**

Visit National Geographic Learning online at **ELTNGL.com**
Visit our corporate website at **www.cengage.com**

Printed in the United Kingdom by Ashford Colour Press
Print Number: 01 Print Year: 2022

Imagine¹ WORKBOOK

A Match.

four   three   one   five   two

1   2   3   4   5   6   7   8   9   10

nine   eight   six   ten   seven

B Count and circle.

1.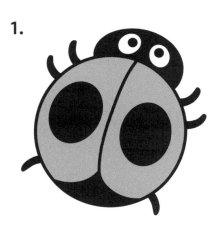

2.

3.

one / (two)   four / five   seven / eight

C Match.

1. What's your name?   a. I'm fine, thanks.

2. How old are you?   b. My name's Han.

3. How are you?   c. I'm seven.

D Write about you.

1. What's your name?   _____

2. How old are you?   _____

3. How are you?   _____

E Listen and number. TR: 0.1

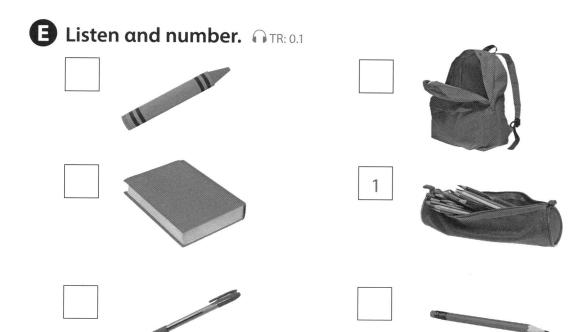

F Read and draw.

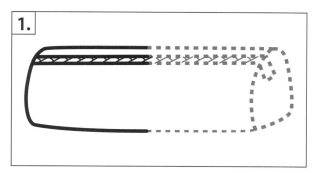

1.

What's this?
It's a pencil case.

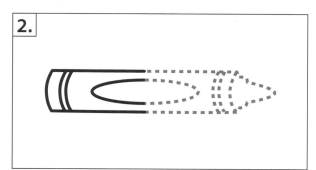

2.

What's this?
It's a crayon.

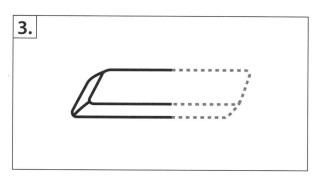

3.

What's this?
It's a rubber.

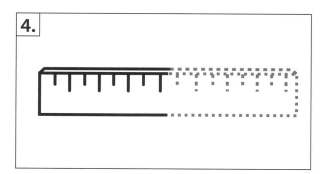

4.

What's this?
It's a ruler.

Lesson 1 Vocabulary

A Circle.

1.

(plane)/ train

2.

game / kite

3.

ball / bat

4.

doll / teddy

B Match.

1.

2.

3.

4.

| bat | game | teddy | train |

C Listen. Write a tick (✓) or a cross (✗). 🎧 TR: 1.1

1. ✓

2. ☐

3. ☐

4. ☐

5. ☐

6. ☐

A **Listen, read and circle.** Then colour the teddy. TR: 1.2

This is my ball.
The / **This** is my plane.
This **a** / **is** my bat.
This is **my** / **one** train.

This is my doll.
And / **This** is my kite.
This **is** / **to** my teddy.
It's brown and white.

B **Read and draw.**

1.
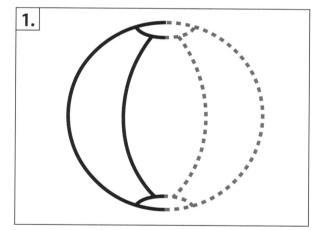
This is my ball.

3.
This is my doll.

2.
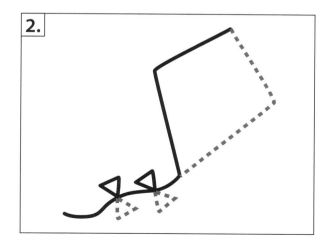
This is my kite.

4.
This is my plane.

A Circle the word for a toy.

favourite   fun   ⟨marble⟩

B Read and circle. 🎧 TR: 1.3

Look at the photo. This is a game of marbles. Marbles is my favourite ⟨game⟩/ **play**. It's fun!

A marble is small. It's a small **ball** / **colour**.

Find a blue marble. Find a red and white **game** / **marble**. Find a yellow marble. Yellow is my favourite **colour** / **marble**. Is this your **favourite** / **fun** colour too?

C Read again. Colour the marbles.

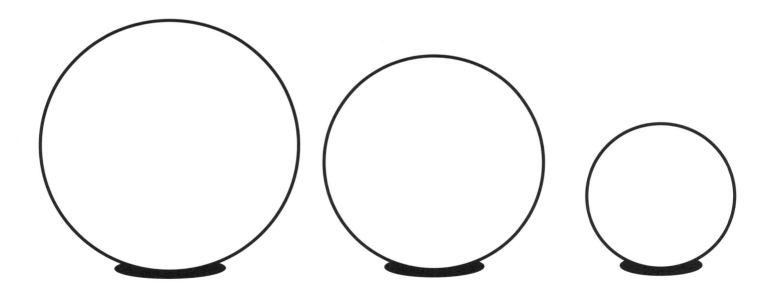

A Read and tick (✓).

Tom

1.

Is this your bat, Tom?

✓ Yes, it is.

☐ No, it isn't.

3.

Is this your teddy, Tom?

☐ Yes, it is.

☐ No, it isn't.

2.
Is this your ball, Tom?

☐ Yes, it is.

☐ No, it isn't.

4.

Is this your plane, Tom?

☐ Yes, it is.

☐ No, it isn't.

B Listen and number. Then tick (✓). 🎧 TR: 1.4

☐ Yes, it is.

☐ No, it isn't.

☐ Yes, it is.

☐ No, it isn't.

☐ Yes, it is.

☐ No, it isn't.

1

☐ Yes, it is.

✓ No, it isn't.

A Trace and write.

Aa
apple

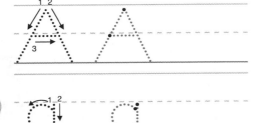

Bb
bag

Cc
carrot

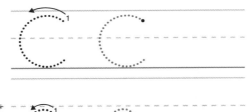

Dd
desk

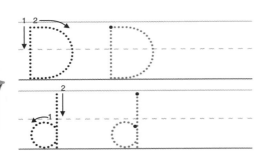

Ee
elephant

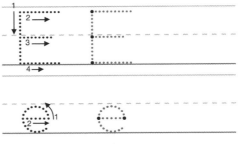

Ff
fish

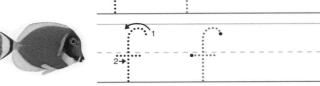

Gg
goat

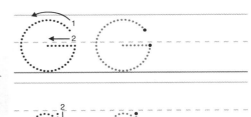

Hh
horse

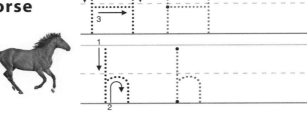

B Listen. Circle the first letter. 🎧 TR: 1.5

1. a　ⓑ　c　d
2. a　b　c　d
3. a　b　c　d

4. e　f　g　h
5. e　f　g　h
6. e　f　g　h

VALUE

Share your toys.

A **Who shares their toys?** Look and tick (✓).

1.

3.

2.

4.

B Read and draw.

I share my toys.

A Match.

| dad | mum | grandma | grandpa |

B Listen and number. TR: 2.1

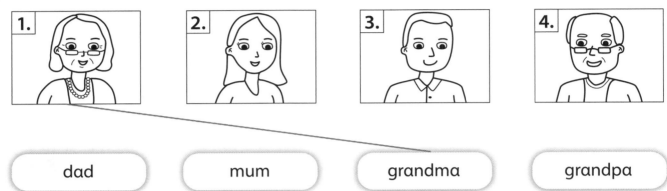

C Read and draw.

This is my family.

A **Listen, read and circle.** 🎧TR: 2.2

(I've got) / **I haven't got** two brothers and a sister too.
I've got / **I haven't got** a cousin. What about you?

I've got / **I haven't got** two grandmas and a grandpa too.
I've got / **I haven't got** an uncle. What about you?

B **Read.** Write a tick (✓) or a cross (✗).

1. I've got a mum and a dad.

2. I haven't got a cousin.

3. I've got a grandma. I haven't got a grandpa.

4. I've got an uncle. I haven't got an aunt.

aunt	
cousin	
dad	
grandma	
grandpa	
mum	✓
uncle	

A Number.

1. boy
2. bus
3. children
4. girl

1

B Read and circle. TR: 2.3

Look at the photo. It's the Mayes family.

They've got a **bus / car** called Skoolie! It's **small / big**. The bus is cool!

Can you see **Dad / Mum**? Her name is Debbie. She's happy! Can you see **Dad / Mum**? His name is Gabriel. He's happy too.

Count the **children / boys**. One, two, three, four. Two boys and two girls. It's a **small / fun** family!

C Read again and match.

1. Skoolie is   a. Dad.

2. Gabriel is   b. a bus.

3. Debbie and Gabriel have got   c. fun family.

4. It's a   d. four children.

A Read and tick (✓).

1. ☐ Her name is Chris.
   ✓ His name is Chris.

2. ☐ Her name is Lee.
   ☐ His name is Lee.

3. ☐ Her name is Nicky.
   ☐ His name is Nicky.

4. ☐ Her name is Pat.
   ☐ His name is Pat.

B Listen and match. 🎧 TR: 2.4

1.   2.   3.   4.

baby sister   cousin   grandpa   mum

Alice   Joe   Pam   Robert

C Read, circle and write. Then draw.

This is my friend.
His / Her name is

_____ .

A Trace and write.

Ii
insect

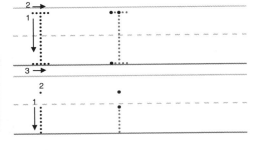

Mm
mum

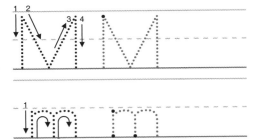

Jj
jellyfish

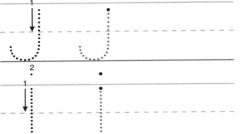

Nn
nose

Kk
kiwi

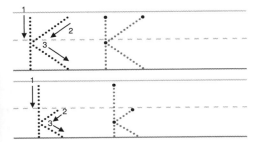

Oo
orange

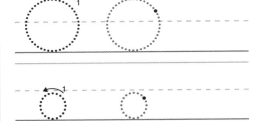

Ll
lamp

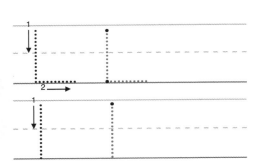

Pp
pencil

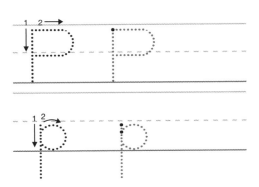

B **Listen.** Circle the first letter. 🎧 TR: 2.5

1. i   j   k   (l)
2. i   j   k   l
3. i   j   k   l

4. m   n   o   p
5. m   n   o   p
6. m   n   o   p

Love your family.

A **Who loves his / her family?** Look and tick (✓).

1. [ ]    [ ]

2. [ ]    [ ]

3. [ ]    [ ]

B Read and draw.

> **I love my family!**

A Listen, read and circle. 🎧 TR: 2.6

Knock! Knock!

Teacher: (Come) / **Sit** in. Hello, Sam.

Sam: Hello.

Teacher: **Sit** / **Stand** down. OK, boys and girls. **Close** / **Open** your books. Let's read.

Sam: Oh, no! This isn't my English book!

Teacher: **Stand** / **Put** your hand up, Sam.

Sam: Can I look at your book, **please** / **thank you**?

Teacher: Yes, OK.

Teacher: **Close** / **Open** your books now. Time to go home! **Sit** / **Stand** up, boys and girls.

Sam: Here's your book. Goodbye!

Teacher: **Please** / **Thank you**, Sam. Goodbye!

B Read and tick (✓).

1.
   - [✓] Put your hand up.
   - [ ] Stand up.

3.
   - [ ] Come in.
   - [ ] Please.

2.
   - [ ] Open your books.
   - [ ] Thank you.

4.
   - [ ] Close your books.
   - [ ] Sit down.

A **Remember.** Tick (✓) the toys in the video.

☐ ☐ ☐ ☐ ☐

B **Draw a sign for the toy museum.**

Toy
Museum

C **You're at the museum now.** Draw and colour your favourite toy.
Read and circle.

It's my favourite toy. It's **big** / **small**.

A **Find and circle people in the family.**

1.	s	f	g	m	u	m	h	l
2.	g	r	a	n	d	m	a	i
3.	j	g	r	a	n	d	p	a
4.	f	u	n	c	l	e	x	d
5.	d	b	a	b	y	l	n	r
6.	g	r	c	o	u	s	i	n

B **Look and write.**

1.   l o d l

    d o l l

2.   l e p n a

    _ _ _ _ _

3.   r n a t i

    _ _ _ _ _

4.   a g e m

    _ _ _ _

C **Circle the first letter.**

1.  **i** / **o** nsect

2.  **p** / **c** arrot

3. 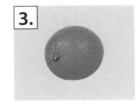 **o** / **i** range

4. 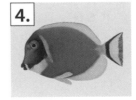 **d** / **f** ish

5. 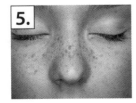 **m** / **n** ose

6.  **h** / **f** orse

7.  **c** / **g** oat

8.  **j** / **l** amp

D Read and match.

1.

Is this your kite, Tom?

2.

Is this your book, Tom?

3.

What's this, Anna?

It's a ball.

It's a train.

No, it isn't.

No, it isn't.

Yes, it is.

Yes, it is.

4.

What's this, Tom?

5.

Is this your bag, Anna?

6.

Is this your pencil case, Anna?

E Read and circle.

1. I've got a baby (**brother**) / **sister**. His name is Tom.

2. I've got an **aunt** / **uncle**. Her name is Rita.

3. I've got a **grandma** / **grandpa**. His name is Charlie.

4. I've got a **mum** / **dad**. Her name is Nicole.

5. I've got an **aunt** / **uncle**. She's my mum's sister.

6. My uncle and aunt have got a baby. He's my **cousin** / **brother**.

3 Homes

A Circle.

1.

bed / cupboard

2.

shower / TV

3.

bed / shower

4.

cupboard / TV

B Number.

1. bathroom
2. bedroom
3. kitchen
4. living room

C Listen and number. TR: 3.1

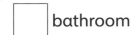 bathroom

 bedroom

1 kitchen

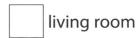 living room

22

A **Listen, read and circle.** 🎧 TR: 3.2

(**Where's**)/ **Where** the bed?
Where is it?
The bed's **in** / **it** the bedroom.
Jump on it!

Where / **Where's** the sofa?
Where is it?
The sofa's **it** / **in** the living room.
Sit on it!

B **Read and draw.**

A: Where's the lamp?

B: It's in the bedroom.

A: Where's Mum?

B: She's in the living room.

A: Where's the shower?

B: It's in the bathroom.

A: Where's the cupboard?

B: It's in the kitchen.

A Match.

1. 2. 3.

clock   house   water

B Read and circle. 🎧 TR: 3.3

Look at the photo. This is a **bathroom** / **bedroom**. It isn't in a house. It's under the **bus** / **water**. Can you see the table? The table is next to the **bed** / **chair**. It's white. The clock is on the table. It's small. The **game** / **train** is on the bed. It's yellow, red and blue. The toy fish are **in** / **on** the bed too.

Look at the fish in the water. They're **big** / **small**!

C Read again and match.

1. The bedroom isn't   a. the table.

2. The bed is next to   b. in a house.

3. The game is red,   c. blue and yellow.

4. The toy fish   d. are on the bed.

A Read and circle.

1. The boy is **next to** / **on** / **under** the sofa.

2. The clock is **next to** / **on** / **under** the photo.

3. The train is **next to** / **on** / **under** the sofa.

4. The photo is **next to** / **on** / **under** the table.

5. The lamp is **next to** / **on** / **under** the TV.

B Listen and circle. 🎧 TR: 3.4

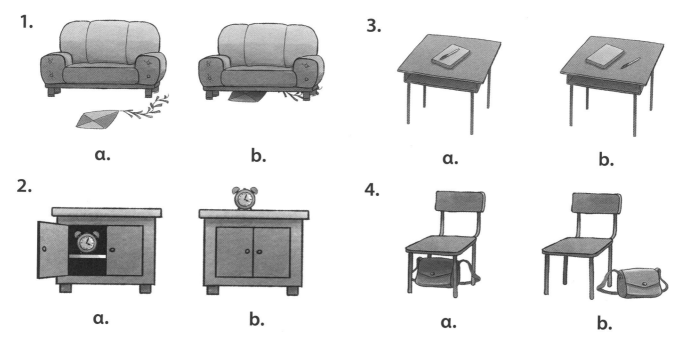

A Trace and write.

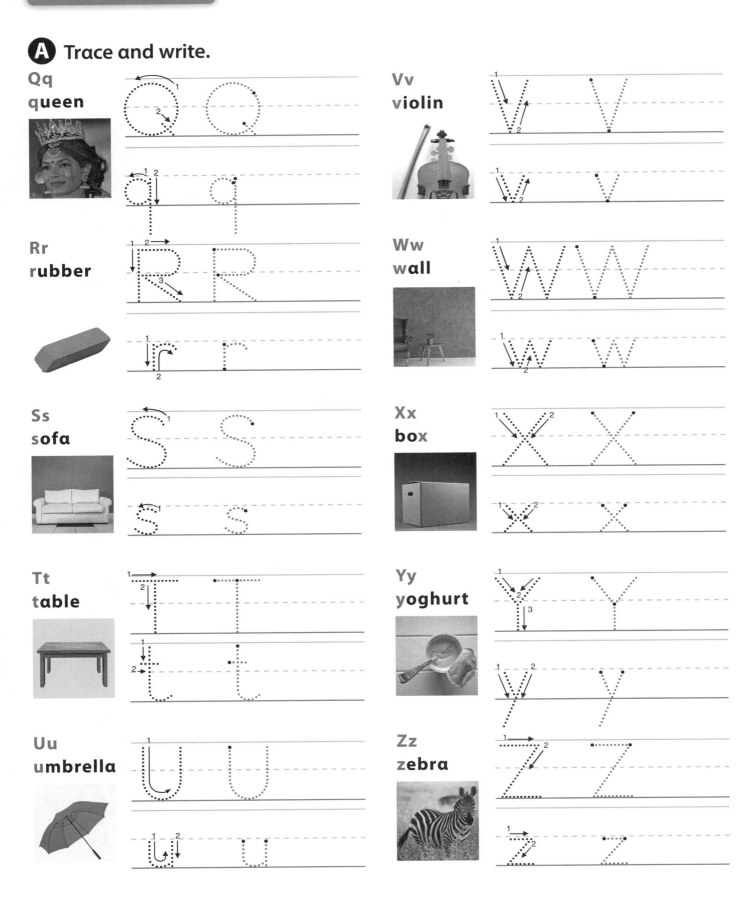

Qq
queen

Rr
rubber

Ss
sofa

Tt
table

Uu
umbrella

Vv
violin

Ww
wall

Xx
box

Yy
yoghurt

Zz
zebra

VALUE

Play with your friends.

A Who plays with their friends? Look and tick (✔).

1. ✔

2.

B Read and draw.

I play with my friends.

4 My Town

A Match.

 1.
 2.
 3.
 4.

| park | playground | shop | zoo |

B Write. library ~~street~~ swimming pool town centre

 1.

street

 3.

 2.

 4.

C Listen and number. 🎧 TR: 4.1

☐ library ☐ shop ☐ swimming pool ☐ zoo

A **Listen, read and write.** TR: 4.2

There's _a_ street, a street,
a street in the town.

_____ _____ shop, a shop,
a shop in the street.

_____ _____ girl, a girl,
a girl _____ the shop.

_____ _____ shop, a shop,
a shop _____ _____ street.

_____ _____ street, a street,
a street _____ _____ _____.

B **Write.**

the park / in / a playground / there's
There's a playground in the park.

there's / the shop / in / a man

_____

a library / in / there's / the street

_____

A Write.

| model   real   tiny |

1.

model

2.

_____

3.

_____

B Read and write. TR: 4.3

| model   real   tiny   town   trees |

Look at the photo! It's a ____town____.
Is it a real town? No, it isn't. It's a
_____ . The houses and shops
are small. They're _____!

There's a boy. He's real. There are
_____ too. They're small. Are
they _____? Yes, they are.

Look at the cars. Are they big or
small? They're small. They aren't real.
They're models. This model town is cool!

C Read again. Write T (true) or F (false).

1. This town is real. ☐

2. The houses are big. ☐

3. The shops are small. ☐

4. This is a real boy. ☐

5. The trees are real. ☐

6. This town is cool. ☐

A Read and write.

1. ___There's___ a shop in the street.

2. _____ trees in the park.

3. _____ books in the library.

4. _____ a man in the swimming pool.

B Listen and circle. 🎧 TR: 4.4

1.

    a.   b.

3.

    a.   b.

2.

    a.   b.

4.

    a.   b.

A Tick (✓) the words with a.

1. ✓
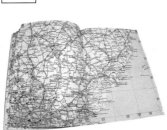

2. ☐
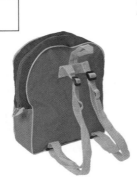

3. ☐

4. ☐

B Write.

1.

j _a_ m

2.

m __ n

3.

m __ p

4.

b __ t

C Listen and write the words with a. 🎧 TR: 4.5

1. b a t

2. __ __ __

3. __ __ __

4. __ __ __

5. __ __ __

6. __ __ __

VALUE

Love your town.

A **Who loves their town?** Write *Yes* or *No*.

1. _____No_____

2. _____

3. _____

4. _____

5. _____

B Write and draw.

> **This is me. Look! I'm in my town. I _____ my town.**

A Do the crossword.

Across →

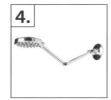

Down ↓

A **Remember.** Tick (✓) the animals in the video.

☐ ☐ ☐ ☐

B **Look at the animals.** Draw the tails.

C **You're in Africa now.** Draw and colour your favourite animal. Read and circle.

This is my favourite animal. It's **big / small**.

A **Find and circle.** Then write.

1.

2.

3.

p	a	s	t	r	e	e	t
k	k	i	t	c	h	e	n
s	l	i	b	r	a	r	y
w	a	s	h	o	w	e	r
h	u	b	s	h	o	p	e
b	e	d	r	o	o	m	v

4.

5.

6.

B **Circle the odd one out.**

1. cupboard | bed | (zoo)

2. living room | street | town centre

3. TV | playground | kitchen

C **Remember the sounds.** Listen and circle the odd one out. 🎧 TR: 4.6

1.

   a.　　　　b.　　　　(c.)

2.

   a.　　　　b.　　　　c.

3.

   a.　　　　b.　　　　c.

4.

   a.　　　　b.　　　　c.

D Look and match.

1. Where's the umbrella?

2. Where's the book?

3. Where's the ball?

4. Where's the doll?

5. Where's the plane?

a. It's on the table.

b. It's under the table.

c. It's next to the table.

d. It's on the sofa.

e. It's under the sofa.

E Read and draw.

Look! There are two children in the park. The boy is under the tree. He's got a book. The girl is next to the woman. She's her mum. The girl has got an apple. Look! There are three birds in the sky. One, two, three.

5 On the Farm

A Circle.

chicken / cow   donkey / duck   bee / sheep   bird / dog

B Write.

chicken   dog   donkey   sheep

_____   _____   _____   _____

C Listen and write the animal. 🎧 TR: 5.1

bee   bird   chicken   ~~cow~~   dog   donkey   duck   sheep

1. _____cow_____   5. _____

2. _____   6. _____

3. _____   7. _____

4. _____   8. _____

A **Listen, read and write.** TR: 5.2

A dog _____ run,
but a dog _____ talk.

A cat _____ swim,
but a cat _____ walk.

A bird _____ sing,
and a bird _____ fly.

A bird _____ fly very,
very high.

B **Read and tick (✓).**

1.

It can run, but it can't fly.

2.

It can swim and fly, but it can't
talk.

3.

It can fly, but it can't jump.

4.

It can fly and walk, but it
can't swim.

C **Write.**

I can _____.

I can't _____.

A **Write.**

> farmer   food   pen

1.

2.
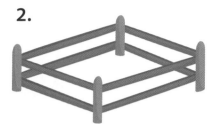

3.

_____   _____   _____

B **Read and write.** 🎧 TR: 5.3

> boy   farmer   food   school   sheep

Can you play with animals at school? No! You can play with your friends at _____ . Can you play with animals on a farm? Yes! Look at this farm.

This is a pen. It's a _____ pen. A pen is a sheep's 'house'. Look! Can you see the _____ ? She's got _____ for the sheep.

Look at the _____ ! He's got food for the sheep too.

C **Read again and circle.**

1. You **can** / (**can't**) play with animals at school.

2. You **can** / **can't** play with your friends at school.

3. A sheep's house is a **pen** / **pencil**.

4. The farmer has got food for the **boy** / **sheep**.

A **Read and circle.**

1. Can a bird fly?

   Yes, it can. / No, it can't.

2. Can a dog jump?

   Yes, it can. / No, it can't.

3. Can a donkey fly?

   Yes, it can. / No, it can't.

4. Can a chicken draw a picture?

   Yes, it can. / No, it can't.

5. Can a cat run?

   Yes, it can. / No, it can't.

B **Write.** Then listen and check. 🎧 TR: 5.4

(read)

Can a duck read?

No, it can't.

(fly)

(jump)

(swim)

A Tick (✓) the words with *e*.

1. ✓
2. ☐
3. ☐
4. ☐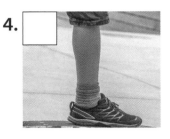

5. ☐
6. ☐
7. ☐
8. ☐

B Write.

1.    l __ g
2. 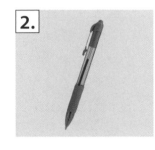   p __ n
3.    b __ d
4.    t __ n

C Listen and write the words with *e*. ⌒ TR: 5.5

1. __ __ __

2. __ __ __

3. __ __ __

4. __ __ __

5. __ __ __

6. __ __ __

VALUE

Be kind to animals.

A **Who's kind to animals?** Write *Yes* or *No*.

1. _____Yes_____   4. _____

2. _____   5. _____

3. _____   6. _____

B Read and draw.

> ## This is me. Look! I'm kind to animals.

Lesson 1 Vocabulary

A **What is it?** Circle.

1. shoes / (T-shirt)

2. dress / trousers

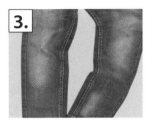

3. jeans / socks

4. shirt / skirt

B **Look and write.** Use words from Activity A.

1. shirt

2. _____

3. _____

4. _____

C **Listen and colour.** 🎧 TR: 6.1

A Listen, read and write. TR: 6.2

Is this your shirt? Is this your shirt?
Yes, it _____. This is my shirt.

_____ this your hat? Is _____ your hat?
No, it _____. This isn't my hat.

Are these your shoes? Are these your shoes?
No, they _____. These aren't my shoes.

Are _____ your socks? Are these your socks?
Yes, they _____. These are my socks.

B Read and circle.

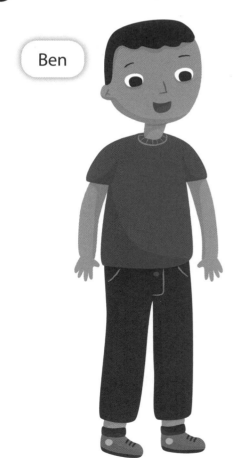

Ben

1.

A: Is this your
T-shirt, Ben?

B: Yes, it is. /
No, it isn't.

2.

A: Are these your
shoes, Ben?

B: Yes, they are. /
No, they aren't.

3.

A: Are these your
socks, Ben?

B: Yes, they are. /
No, they aren't.

4.

A: Are these your
trousers, Ben?

B: Yes, they are. /
No, they aren't.

A Match.

1. 2. 3. 4. 5.

(boots)　(gloves)　(happy)　(hat)　(scarecrow)

B Read and write. 🎧 TR: 6.3

(blue　face　farms　hat　real　shoes)

Look at this man. Is he _____? No, he isn't.
He's a scarecrow. A scarecrow is a big doll. You can see
scarecrows on _____.

This scarecrow is happy. Look at his mouth! He's got big
eyes. What colour is his _____? It's orange.

What about his clothes? He's got a _____
and red shirt and jeans. He hasn't got _____,
but he's got boots. They're black. He's got a nice
_____ and two gloves.

Can you make a scarecrow?

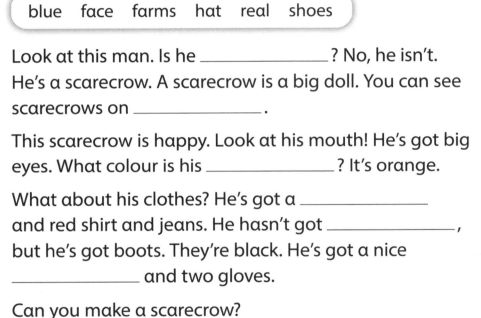

C Read again. Write T (true) or F (false).

1. A scarecrow is a small doll. ☐

2. You can see scarecrows on farms. ☐

3. This scarecrow has got a blue face. ☐

4. He's got blue boots. ☐

5. He's got gloves on his hands. ☐

A **Read and match.**

1. What colour is the sky?   a. They're orange.

2. What colour is the sun?   b. It's yellow.

3. What colour are lemons?   c. They're yellow.

4. What colour are carrots?   d. It's blue.

B **Listen and colour.** Then write. 🎧 TR: 6.4

1. His _____ is yellow.   5. His _____ blue.

2. His _____ are brown.   6. _____ red.

3. His _____ black.   7. _____ orange.

4. His _____ green.

A Tick (✓) the words with *i*.

1.  ✓

2.

3.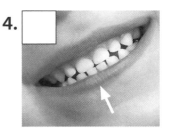

4.

5.

6.

7.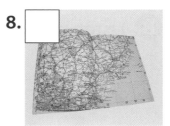

8.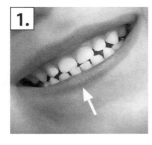

B Write.

1.

l __ p

2.

s __ t

3.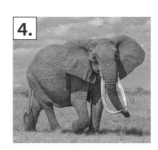

s __ x

4.

b __ g

C Listen and write the words with *i*. 🎧 TR: 6.5

1. __ __ __

2. __ __ __

3. __ __ __

4. __ __ __

5. __ __ __

6. __ __ __

VALUE

Wear clean clothes.

A Who wears clean clothes? Look and tick (✓).

1.

2.

3.

4.

5.

6.

B Read and draw.

> ## This is me. Look! I wear clean clothes.

A **Listen, read and circle.** 🎧 TR: 6.6

Sam: Hi, Rosa.

Rosa: Hi, Sam. Let's work **together** / **on**.

Sam: Where's the activity?

Rosa: It's on page 7. It's Activity 2.

Sam: Thank you. Let's **take** / **have** turns. You first. What's number 1?

Rosa: It's a sofa. Can we write the answers in the book?

Sam: Yes.

Rosa: Can I **borrow** / **show** a pencil?

Sam: Yes, **there** / **here**.

Rosa: Thank you. Oh, no! This isn't correct. Please **have** / **pass** the rubber.

Sam: OK. It's **me** / **my** turn. Number 2. This is a shower.

Rosa: Yes!

B **Read and tick (✓).**

1. Let's work together.

2. Let's take turns.

3. Can I borrow a ruler?

✓ OK. Let's take turns.	☐ OK. You first.	☐ It's on page 10.
☐ No, you first.	☐ Please pass the ruler.	☐ Yes, here.

A Remember the video. Match.

bag   doll   market   mask

B Draw some things in a market.

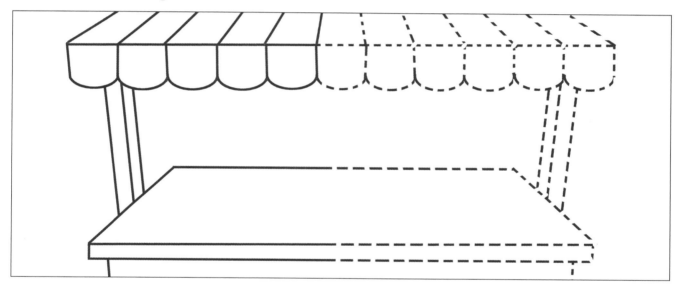

C You're at the market now.
Draw your favourite bag.
Read and circle.

This is my favourite bag.
It's **big / small**.

A Find and circle. Then write.

1.

2.

3.

4.

s	h	e	e	p	n	s	h
t	r	o	u	s	e	r	s
m	i	d	o	n	k	e	y
j	e	s	h	i	r	t	a
n	d	o	g	k	o	a	s
d	r	s	h	o	e	s	g
c	d	o	s	o	c	k	s
b	i	r	d	z	e	l	a

5.

6.

7.

8.

B Circle the odd one out.

1. T-shirt — socks — duck

2. dress — cow — bee

3. bird — jeans — skirt

4. shoes — chicken — shirt

5. dog — donkey — trousers

C Write *e* or *i*.

1.
b _i_ g

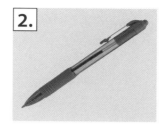
2.
p __ n

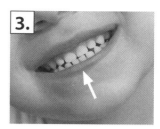
3.
l __ p

4.
b __ d

5.
s __ x

6.
l __ g

D Match.

1. What colour is his hat?
2. Are these your shoes?
3. Can you see the dog?
4. Is this your skirt?
5. What colour are her socks?
6. Can a duck talk?

a. They're pink.
b. No, they aren't.
c. Yes, it is.
d. It's brown.
e. No, it can't.
f. Yes, I can.

E Listen. Write a tick (✓) or a cross (✗). ⌒ TR: 6.7

	swim	sing	fly a kite
1. Marcel	✗		
2. AJ			
3. Yurara			
4. Kaitlyn			

7 Let's Eat!

Lesson 1 Vocabulary

A Circle.

1.

lemon / tomato

2.

bread / rice

3.

banana / water

4.

sweet / milk

B Write.

banana   milk   potato   rice

1.

2.

3.

4.

_____   _____   _____   _____

C Listen, number and write. 🎧 TR: 7.1

☐

1

tomato

☐

☐

_____   _____   _____   _____

A Listen, read and write. 🎧 TR: 7.2

I _____ bananas
and I _____ bread.
I _____ apples, green or red!

I _____ oranges
and I _____ rice.
I _____ milk. It isn't very nice!

B Read and number.

1.

I like apples and oranges.
I like water too.
I don't like milk.

☐

a.

2.

I like apples and bananas.
I like milk too.
I don't like oranges.

☐

b.

3.

I like bananas and oranges.
I like water too.
I don't like milk.

1

c.

A **Read and number.**

   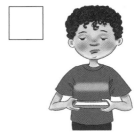

1. This tray is big.

2. This tray is small.

3. This lunch is great.

4. This lunch is horrible.

B **Read and write.** 🎧 TR: 7.3

food   girls   like   lunch   there   trays

Look at the photo. The boys and _____ are at school. It's time for _____ . It's school lunch. They've got _____ . How many trays can you see? There is _____ on the trays. What food can you see?

Look! Is that rice? Yes, it is. And that's cabbage. Yes! And _____ are beans too. Do you _____ rice, beans and cabbage?

C **Read again.** Write T (true) or F (false).

1. It's time for bed. ☐

2. The boys and girls have got boxes. ☐

3. The boys and girls are at school. ☐

4. There is food under the trays. ☐

5. The boys and girls eat rice for lunch. ☐

A Read and write.

It's OK. They're OK. ~~Yes, I do.~~ No, I don't.

1. Do you like bananas?

   <u>Yes, I do.</u> ☺

2. Do you like potatoes?

   _____ 😐

3. Do you like milk?

   _____ 😐

4. Do you like bread?

   _____ ☹

B Listen and draw. 🎧 TR: 7.4

Key
✓ = ☺
– = 😐
✗ = ☹

A Tick (✓) the words with *o*.

1. ✓
2.
3.
4.

5.
6.
7.
8.

B Write.

1.

m __ p

2.

d __ t

3.

d __ g

4.

n __ d

C Listen and write the words with *o*. TR: 7.5

1. __ __ __

2. __ __ __

3. __ __ __

4. __ __ __

5. __ __ __

6. __ __ __

VALUE

Eat good food.

A **What's good food?** Look and tick (✓).

1. ✓

2. ☐

3. ☐

4. ☐

5. ☐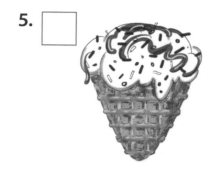

6. ☐

B Read and draw.

Look! I eat good food.

8 At the Beach

Lesson 1 Vocabulary

A Match.

 1.  2.  3.  4.

(boat)   (ice cream)   (sea)   (sun hat)

B Write.

(beach   sand   sandcastle   shell)

 1.  2.  3. 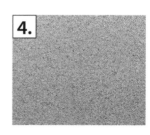 4.

_____   _____   _____   _____

C Listen and write. Then draw. 🎧 TR: 8.1

1.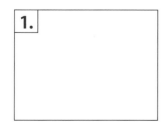

2.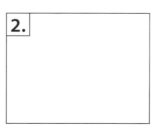

3.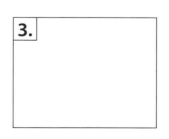

4.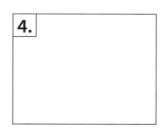

<u>b</u> <u>o</u> <u>a</u> <u>t</u>   _ _ _ _ _ _   _ _ _ _ _ _   _ _ _ _

A **Listen, read and write.** 🎧 TR: 8.2

_____ a beach ball in the sea.
_____ beach balls, one, two, three!

_____ a sun hat on my head.
_____ sun hats, blue or red.

B **Read and number.**

1. There aren't shells.

2. There isn't a sandcastle.

3. There aren't sun hats.

4. There isn't a teddy.

A Match.

breathe

mask

snorkel

B Read and write. 🎧 TR: 8.3

boat   fish   holiday   masks   sea   water

It's _____ time! The sun is in the sky.
It's a nice day.

These two children aren't at school. Look!
They're in the _____. But they aren't in
a _____. They're in the water.

The children can see. They've got _____
on their faces. They can breathe under the
_____ too. They've got snorkels.

Are there _____ in the water?
Yes, there are! Look! How many fish can you see?

C Read again. Write Yes or No.

1. Are the children at school? _____No_____

2. Are the children in the sea? _____

3. Are the children in a boat? _____

4. Can the children see under the water? _____

5. Can the children breathe under the water? _____

A Read and write.

Kai: _____ there a beach in your town?

Emma: No, there _____ .

Kai: I see. _____ there an ice cream shop?

Emma: Yes, there _____ !

Kai: Great! And _____ there sweet shops?

Emma: No, there _____ .

B Listen and draw. 🎧 TR: 8.4

A Tick (✓) the words with *u*.

1.
2.
3.
4.

5.
6.
7.
8.

B Write.

1.

c __ p

2.

m __ m

3.

b __ s

4.

r __ n

C Listen and write the words with *u*. 🎧 TR: 8.5

1. __ __ __

2. __ __ __

3. __ __ __

4. __ __ __

5. __ __ __

6. __ __ __

VALUE

Play outside in the sun.

A Who plays outside in the sun? Look and tick (✓).

1.

2. ✓

3.

4.

5.

6.

B Read and draw.

Look! I play outside in the sun.

A Do the crossword.

Down ↓

Across →

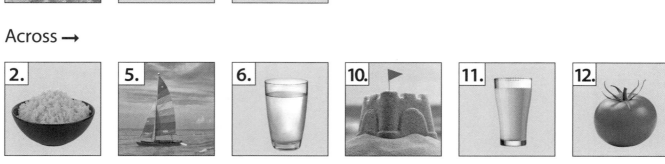

A **Remember the video.** Match.

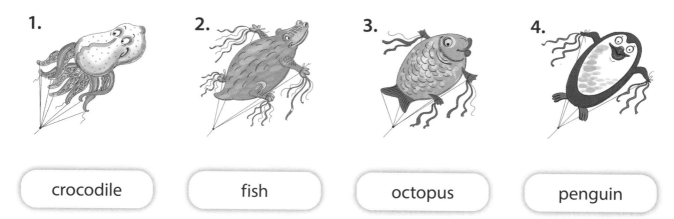

(crocodile) (fish) (octopus) (penguin)

B **Draw an animal kite.**

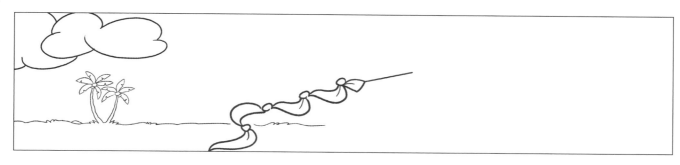

C **You're at the kite festival now.** Draw and colour your favourite kite. Read and circle.

This is my favourite kite. It's **big** / **small**.

A Read and draw.

Look! This is a picture of me at the beach. There is a sandcastle next to me. There are two shells on the sandcastle! There is a toy boat next to me. There is a beach ball on the sand too.

B Look. Write B (beach) or F (food).

1. shell _____B_____

2. beach ball _____

3. rice _____

4. banana _____

5. sand _____

6. sun hat _____

7. sweet _____

8. bread _____

9. potato _____

C Look and colour.

Words with:

a = green   e = blue   i = red   o = yellow   u = orange

D Listen and draw. 🎧 TR: 8.6

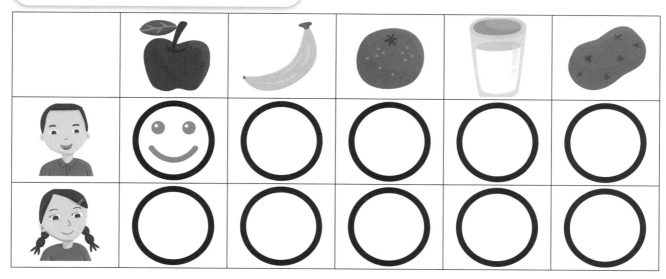

Key

✓ = 😊   − = 😐   ✗ = 🙁

E Circle.

Yara: Let's **go** / **play** to the beach!

Emma: Great idea! **Are** / **Is** there sand?

Yara: Yes, there **is** / **are**.

Emma: **Are** / **Is** there shells?

Yara: **Yes** / **No**, there are.

Emma: Are there boats?

Yara: No, there **aren't** / **are**.

Emma: Is there an ice cream shop?

Yara: No, there **isn't** / **aren't**.

Emma: Oh!

Yara: But **there** / **there's** a sweet shop!

Emma: Great!

Word List

Welcome	Unit 1	Unit 2	Unit 3	Unit 4
one	apple	aunt	bathroom	bag
two	bag	baby	bed	bat
three	ball	boy	bedroom	jam
four	bat	bus	box	library
five	carrot	children	clock	man
six	desk	cousin	cupboard	map
seven	doll	dad	house	model
eight	elephant	girl	kitchen	park
nine	favourite	grandma	living room	playground
ten	fish	grandpa	queen	real
bag	fun	insect	rubber	shop
book	game	jellyfish	shower	street
crayon	goat	kiwi	sofa	swimming pool
pen	horse	lamp	table	tiny
pencil	kite	me	TV	town centre
pencil case	marble	mum	umbrella	zoo
rubber	plane	nose	violin	
ruler	teddy	orange	wall	
	train	pencil	water	
		uncle	yoghurt	
			zebra	

Unit 5	Unit 6	Unit 7	Unit 8
bed	big	banana	beach
bee	bin	beans	beach ball
bird	boots	bread	boat
chicken	dress	cabbage	breathe
cow	gloves	dog	bus
dog	happy	dot	cup
donkey	hat	fox	ice cream
duck	jeans	lemon	jug
farmer	lip	lunch	mask
food	scarecrow	milk	mum
leg	shirt	mop	run
pen	shoes	nod	sand
pet	sit	potato	sandcastle
sheep	six	rice	sea
yes	skirt	sweet	shell
	socks	tomato	snorkel
	trousers	tray	sun hat
	T-shirt	water	

CREDITS